C000257528

No Thoughts
Just Possums

Union Square & Co., LLC, is a subsidiary of Sterling Publishing Co., Inc.

ISBN 978-1-4549-4849-0

For information about custom editions, special sales, and premium purchases, please contact specialsales@unionsquareandco.com.

Printed in China

2 4 6 8 10 9 7 5 3 1

unionsquareandco.com

Text by Sylvie

Cover design by Gina Bonanno

Interior design by Gina Bonanno

No Thoughts Just Possums

I am
impossumbly
sad

You are what you eat!
(trash)

I may be stupid

My brain cells
are fighting
for their lives,

and they’re both losing

Well, Well, Well,

if it isn’t the problems
I created for
for myself

Your honor,
what if I am just
a little guy?

Not to self-diagnose,
but something is

You can’t hit rock bottom

if you’ve been there since birth

I am a possum
on a highway
and life is a ten-ton truck
that hasn't quite
seen me yet

YOLO!
(Thankfully)

How am I supposed to
live, laugh, love
in these conditions?

the marbles have
officially been
lost

If you can't handle me
at my worst,

imagine
how I feel.

Life is soup.

I am fork

whoever prayed for
my downfall,
you won.

I am a

factory reject

Must I pay taxes?

Is it not

enough

to be a funny wee guy?

Sorry for being
that way
It will happen again.

Mentally sick,

physically thick!

Being an idiot is a full-time job,

and I'm employee of the month

I'm like a
clown
except
I don't get paid

Mentally I am
playing dead
on the side of a road

Vermin?
I prefer entrepreneurial,
attractively unpredictable,
free-spirited

Me and my multiple unresolved financial problems, mysterious health issues,

and general burgeoning responsibilities

Normalize

being small and furry

with a pointed snout and

a prehensile tail

AAAAAAAAAAAGGGGGGGGGGGHHHHHHHHHHHHH

but I have very short legs

My life improved
considerably
after completely
giving up

Roses are red
Possums are hairy
Life's crushing reality is
deeply scary

In my defense,
I was left
unsupervised

I am but a jester
in life’s court

If being Hot
was a crime
I would have a very
clean record

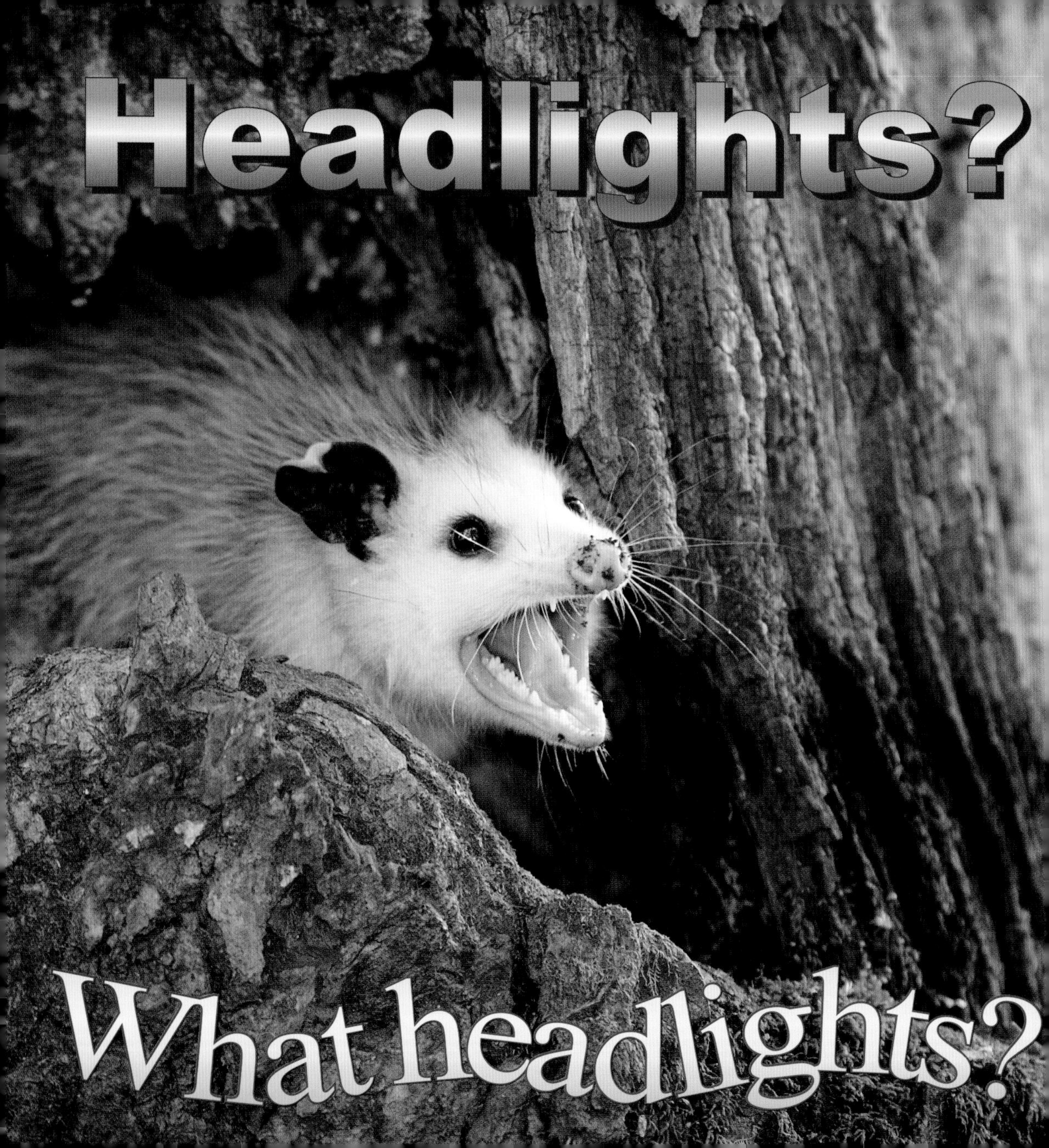
Headlights?
What headlights?

Single by choice

I put the me
in mediocre

I am currently reliving every humiliating moment

I've experienced in my life while trying to sleep

Minimum wage,
maximum rage

The risk I took
was
calculated,
but boy I'm bad at
maths

No Thoughts
Just Possums

Every day
we stray
further from
GOD

If you can't love me at my worst,

I don't blame you

Me neither

Yet again,
I have made
the vibe deeply
awkwardd

I'm also a fool outside of April

I heard you like funny people!

Too many thoughts
head very full

I put the virgin in

Virginia opossum

Are we not all opossums in life's dumpster?

Sick of being the bigger person.
Instead I will crawl into and inhabit
their gutter

I'm just like an opossum (misunderstood and

assumed to be carrying rabies)

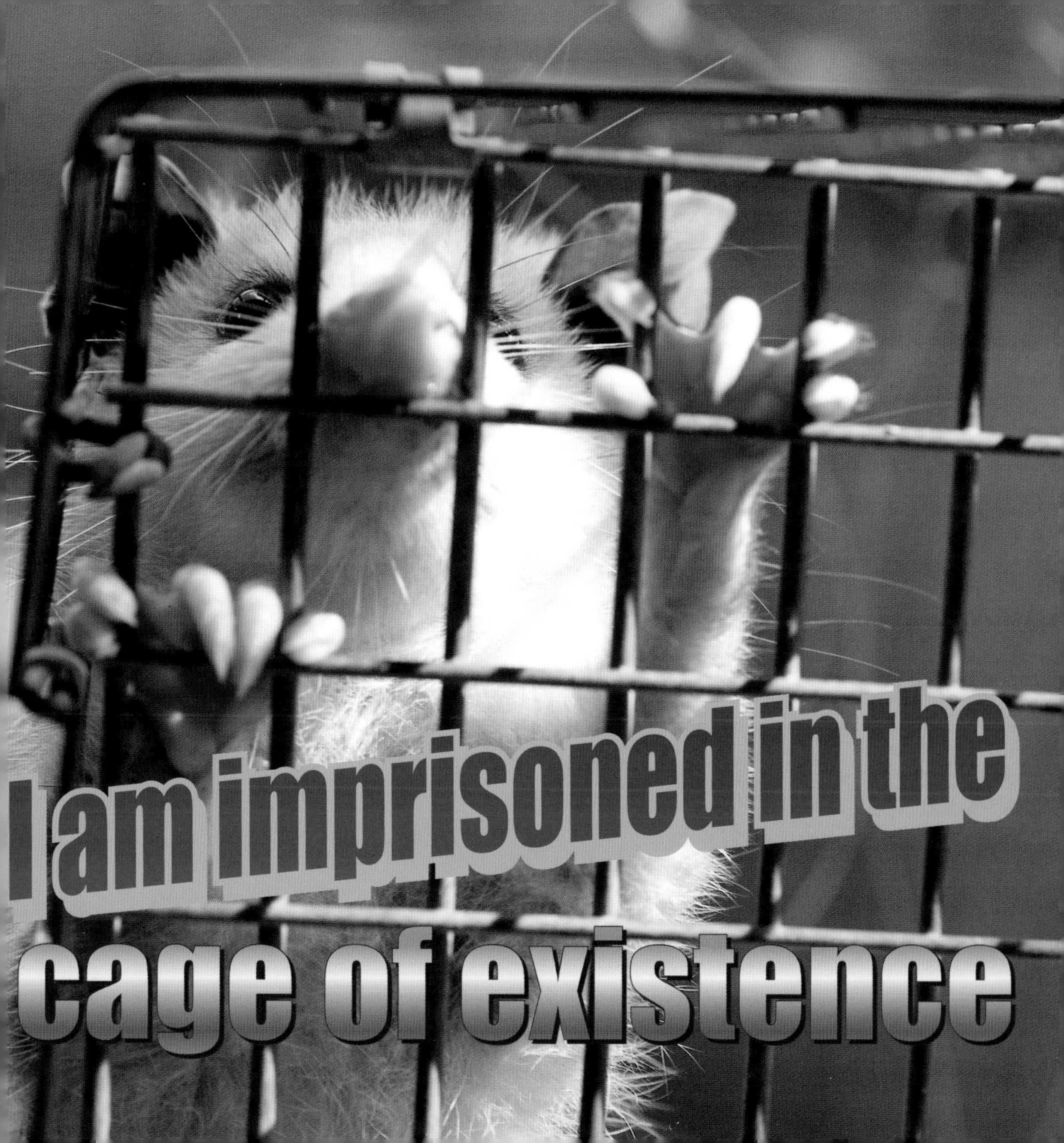
I am imprisoned in the
cage of existence

I put the
happy and
mentally stable
in opossum

Surviving
but certainly not
thriving

Sorry ladies, I'm taken

taken as a joke

Not everything in
this world is bad.
We have opossums

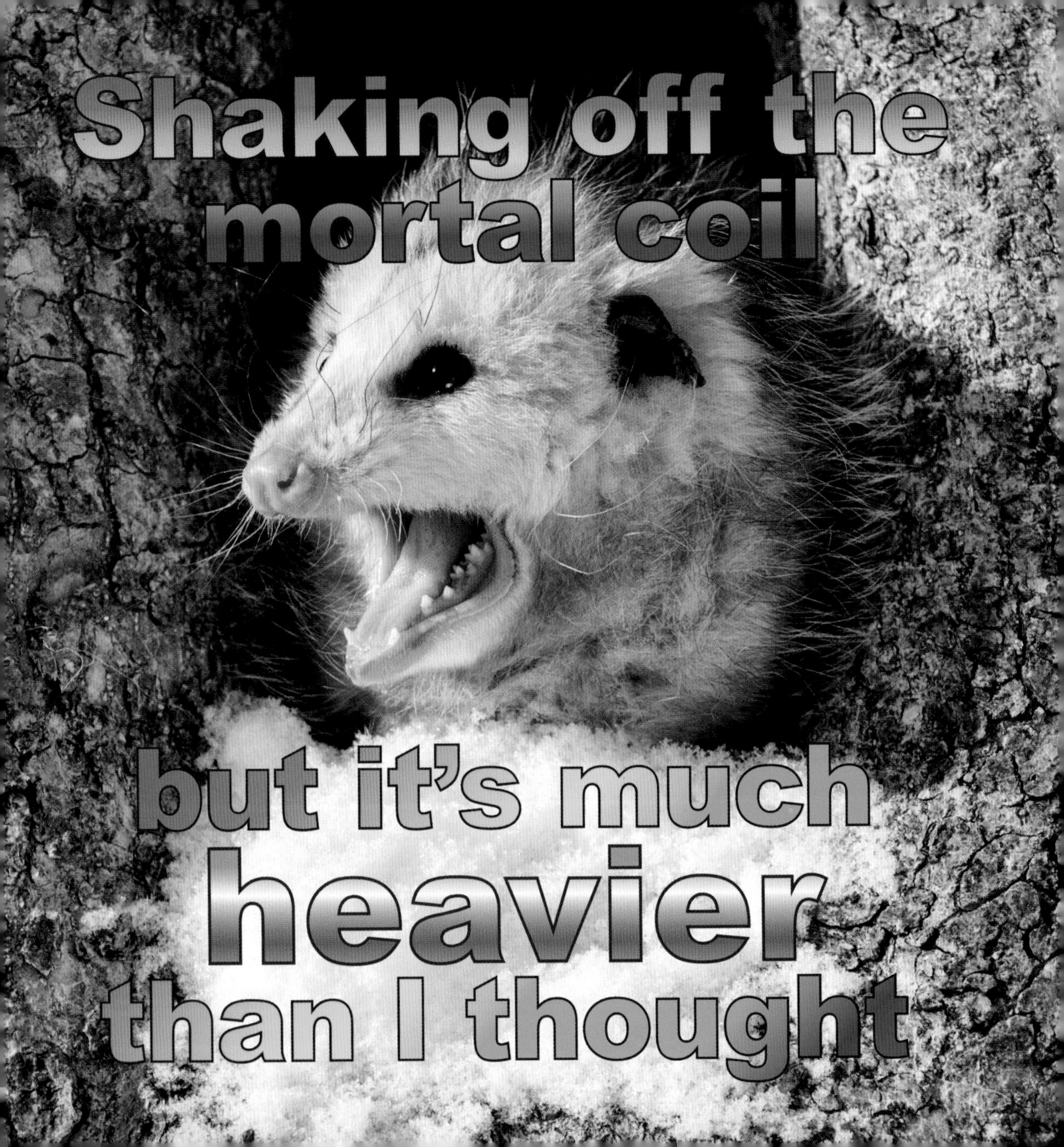

Shaking off the mortal coil

but it’s much heavier than I thought

You should probably
get that checked out...

I have a normal body
with no mysterious
underlying health issues

My life is a
cringe comedy

Opossums are so relatable
I, too, only
come out at night and
eat anything available to me

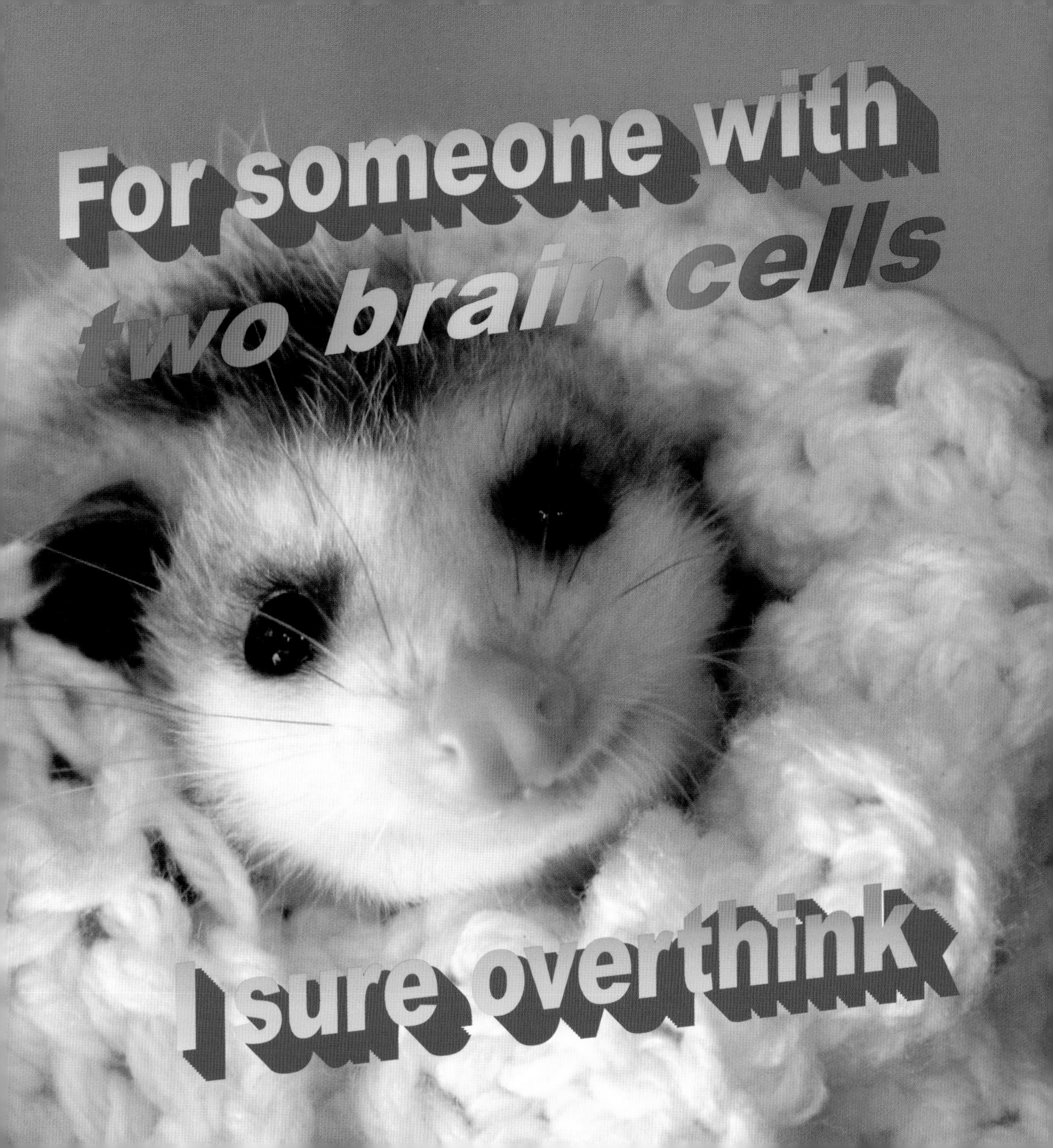

For someone with two brain cells

I sure overthink

Failure
is not an
option

Sorry I was
insane in front of you

do you still think I'm
hot?

Sometimes I think it would be

nice to be an opossum

eating a variety of produce in a

stock image

Like a poss [boss]

My life is less a downward spiral and more a rapid free fall

Being on the Internet

from a young age

has rotted my brain

beyond recognition

Roses are red , alone in my bed
every night i suffer
from existential dread

I am someone's
bowl of cat food
on their porch

and life is an
opportunistic
opossum

They said I could be
anything
so I became a
disappointment

My ancestors really evolved

opossums

All pain
no gain

Crying.

Throwing up.

Eating trash.

Screaming.

Running into traffic.

ME
holding onto
my last shreds of
sanity

Bread
(in French)

Studying
without the
Stu

Reject humanity.
Return to opossum.

I'm one of a kind
but not
in a good way

Too stressed to be blessed

Me and
who

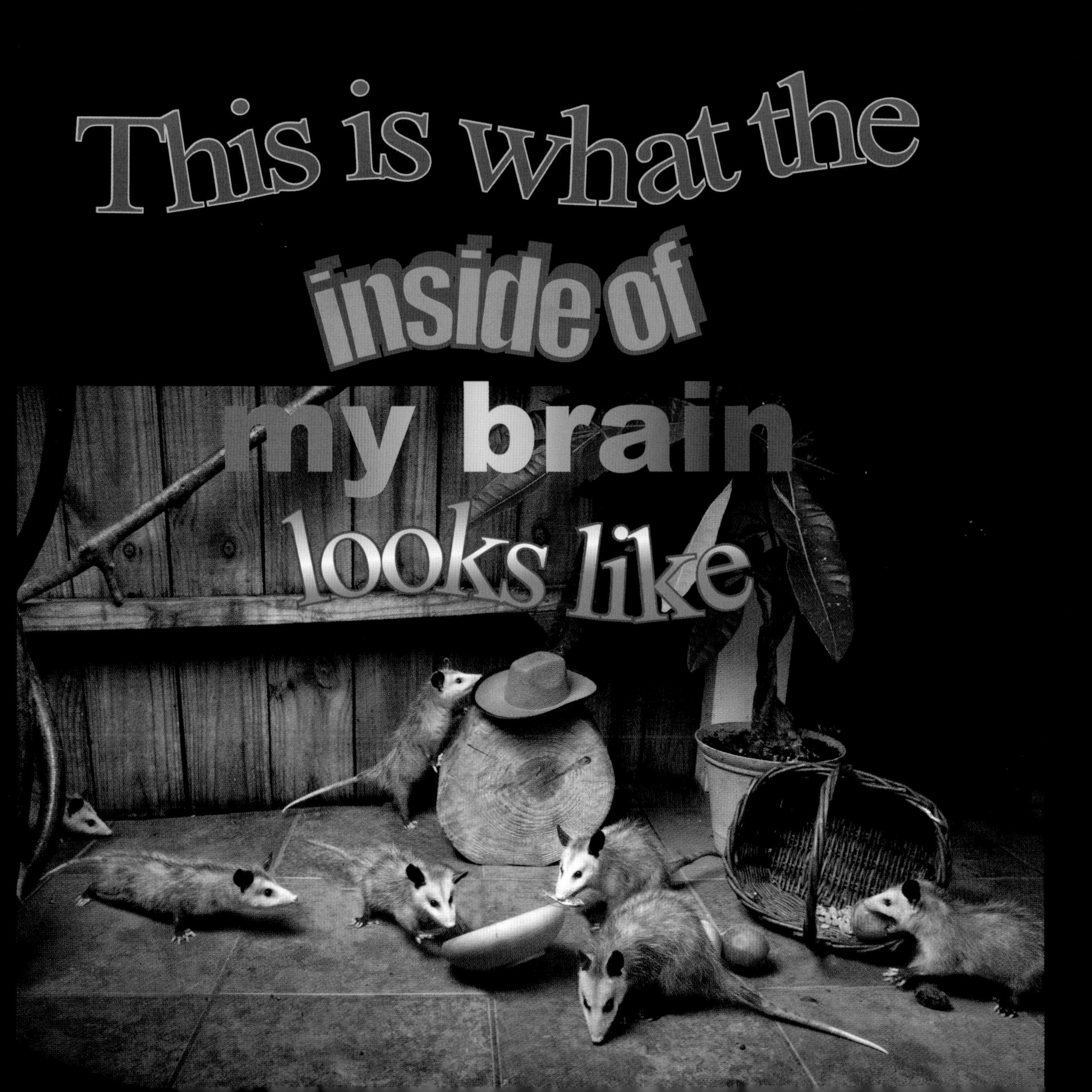
This is what the
inside of
my brain
looks like

Physically sick

Mentally sick
Kind of just sick
all around

I might not look
like much

Life is an
all you can eat buffet
and I'm the last
soggy shrimp
on the plate

A tisket,
a tasket,
I want to be put in
a casket

My demons
are winning

Whoever has my
voodoo
doll
make it stop

I have replaced all ability
to healthily feel
and express emotion
outside of ironic
opossum memes

(Poorly
dressed,
mentally
stressed)

My favorite

party trick

is leaving

Fit is fire

mental state is dire

Cover: rexlis/iStock/Getty Images Plus

Title page: Farinosa/iStock/Getty Images Plus

Copyright page: Farinsa/iStock/Getty Images Plus

I am impossumbly sad: Robert Linder/Unsplash

You are what you eat: Kphotos20/Shutterstock.com

I may be stupid: Dennis Frates/Alamy

My brain cells are fighting for their lives: southeast asia/Alamy

Well, well, well: Farinosa/iStock/Getty Images Plus

Your honor: stanley45/iStock/Getty Images Plus

Not to self-diagnose: tracielouise/iStock/Getty Images Plus

You can't hit rock bottom: Farinosa/iStock/Getty Images Plus

I am a possum: lightstalker/iStock/Getty Images Plus

Yolo: Becky Sheridan/Shutterstock.com

How am I supposed to: UzielGongora/iStock/Getty Images Plus

The marbles have: Moonstone Images/iStock/Getty Images Plus

If you can't handle me: EyeEm/Alamy

Life is soup: carbonero/iStock/Getty Images Plus

Whoever prayed for my downfall: IrinaK/Shutterstock.com

I am a factory reject: ©ludicwaters/Can Stock Photo

Must I pay taxes: Gleive Marcio Rodrigues de Souza/Pexels

Sorry for being that way: chas53/iStock/Getty Images Plus

Mentally sick: Marc Anderson/Alamy

Being an idiot is a full-time job: Mario Hernandez/Pixabay

I'm like a clown: galinast/iStock/Getty Images Plus

Mentally I am playing dead: ScrappinStacy/iStock/Getty Images Plus

Vermin?: irin717/iStock/Getty Images Plus

Me and my multiple unresolved: lilybell/iStock/Getty Images Plus

Normalize being small and furry: timharman/iStock/Getty Images Plus

Aaaargh: johnaudrey/iStock/Getty Images Plus

I am trying to run away: Martin J. Calabrese/iStock/Getty Images Plus

My life improved: Trey Noland/Shutterstock.com

Roses are red: Meli.Stock/Shutterstock.com

In my defense: Weber/iStock/Getty Images Plus

I am but a jester: NajaShots/iStock/Getty Images Plus

If being hot: ChuckSchugPhotography/iStock/Getty Images Plus

Headlights: rexlis/iStock/Getty Images Plus

Single by choice: Photoman195/iStock/Getty Images Plus

I put the me: Shooter1247/iStock/Getty Images Plus

I am currently: rbrucemontgomery/iStock/Getty Images Plus

Minimum wage: NajaShots/iStock/Getty Images Plus

The risk I took: NajaShots/iStock/Getty Images Plus

No thoughts: davidarangod/iStock/Getty Images Plus

Every day we stray: EEI_Tony/iStock/Getty Images Plus

If you can't love: erniedecker/iStock/Getty Images Plus

Yet again: JasonOndreicka/iStock/Getty Images Plus

I'm also a fool: Pleio/iStock/Getty Images Plus

I heard you like funny people: Pleio/iStock/Getty Images Plus

Too many thoughts: Interbober/iStock/Getty Images Plus

I put the virgin in: Rosa Jay/Shutterstock.com

Are we not all opossums: Marianoguiera/iStock/Getty Images Plus

Sick of being the bigger person: bridge99/iStock/Getty Images Plus

I'm just like an opossum: DPLight/iStock/Getty Images Plus

I am imprisoned in the: nebari/iStock/Getty Images Plus

I put the happy: KenCanning/iStock/Getty Images Plus

Surviving: chameleonseye/iStock/Getty Images Plus

Sorry ladies: AMCImages/iStock/Getty Images Plus

Not everything in: Ashley Hutchinson Photography/iStock/Getty Images Plus

Shaking off the: KenCanning/iStock/Getty Images Plus

Inside you there are: Bsheridan1959/iStock/Getty Images Plus

I have a normal body: Bsheridan1959/iStock/Getty Images Plus

My life is a: Bsheridan1959/iStock/Getty Images Plus

Opossums are so relatable: JohnCarnemolla/iStock/Getty Images Plus

For someone with: JoanBudaii/iStock/Getty Images Plus

Failure is not an option: JasonOndreicka/iStock/Getty Images Plus

Sorry I was: Farinosa/iStock/Getty Images Plus

Sometimes I think it would be: irin717/iStock/Getty Images Plus; goir/Shutterstock.com (frame)

Like a poss: Weber/iStock/Getty Images Plus

My life is less a downward spiral: tracielouise/iStock/Getty Images Plus

Being on the internet: Anastasiia Atamanchuk/iStock/Getty Images Plus

Roses are red: tracielouise/iStock/Getty Images Plus

I am someone's bowl of cat food: DLMcK/iStock/Getty Images Plus

They said I could be: Abril Mara/iStock/Getty Images Plus

My ancestors really evolved: Indra Purwibowo/Pexels; carlos Caetano/Shutterstock.com (frame)

All pain: Indra Purwibowo/Pexels

Crying. Throwing Up: Skyler Ewing/Pexels

Me holding onto: daynaw3990/Pixabay

Bread: Phillip w. Kirkland/Shutterstock.com

Studying without stu: LifetimeStock/Shutterstock.com

Reject humanity: Jay Ondreicka/Shutterstock.com

I'm one of a kind: Farinosa/iStock/Getty Images Plus

Too stressed: Donna Racheal/Shutterstock.com

Me and who: Harry Collins Photography/Shutterstock.com

This is what the inside: IrinaK/Shutterstock.com

Physicaly sick: mikeledray/Shutterstock.com

I might not look like much: Evelyn D. Harrison/Shutterstock.com

Life is an all you can eat buffet: Geoffrey Kuchera/Shutterstock.com

A tisket: irin717/iStock/Getty Images Plus

My demons: Kurit afshen/Shutterstock.com

Whoever has my voodoo doll: Jennifer Uppendahl/Unsplash

I have replaced all ability: Jay Ondreicka/Shutterstock.com

Poorly dressed: Nick Pecker/Shutterstock.com

My favorite: Geoffrey Kuchera/Shutterstock.com

Fit is fire: Farinosa/iStock/Getty Images Plus

author photo: Jay Ondreicka/Shutterstock.com

Back cover: Farinosa/iStock/Getty Images Plus

Sylvie is the founder and proprietress of
@69possums420,
a possum meme–focused Instagram account.